CROWOOD EQUESTRIAN GUIDES

Basic Riding

CAROL FOSTER

The Crowood Press

First published in 1991 by
The Crowood Press Ltd
Ramsbury, Marlborough
Wiltshire SN8 2HR

This impression 1992

British Library Cataloguing in Publication Data

Foster, Carol *1952–*
   Basic riding.
   1. Livestock: Horses. Riding
   I. Title
   798.23

ISBN 1 85222 546 2

Acknowledgements:
Line-drawings by Hazel Morgan.
Photographs by Louis Milburn.

Typeset by Footnote Graphics, Warminster, Wiltshire
Printed and bound in Great Britain by BPCC Hazells Ltd
Member of BPCC Ltd

CONTENTS

Most people who learn to ride do so because, from the time they can first remember, a love of horses has played a major part in their lives. Making a detour on the way home from school to pass a field where horses graze, or, better still, getting to know the owner who may allow help with grooming or mucking out, are all part of the pattern from which the keen rider emerges. It is unlikely therefore that the person who arrives, full of anticipation, for his first riding lesson, has never before approached a horse.

If horses are to respect us we must first respect them, and our first approaches should be governed by a set of basic rules which are lent as much to safety and common sense as the respect we should have towards any animal.

Respect comes from understanding how the horse functions and thinks. The horse is, quite naturally, an animal that runs away from danger and is capable of being easily alarmed. Horses have acute hearing (watch how their ears move constantly like antennae, picking up vibrations and sounds around them) so loud voices or worse, shouting, will only trigger off the responses for 'fight or flight' in the horse. With his eyes placed on the side of the head, the horse has a wide range of vision, but if you creep up silently from behind, he might decide to 'fight' or kick and then to 'take flight' or run away. A steady, reassuring, matter-of-fact voice should always be used; it will even give you confidence when you may be feeling a bit nervous! Whether the horse is in a stable or field, walk purposefully towards him, approaching his shoulder. If it is your first time at a riding school, or if you are inexperienced at catching a pony in a field, do not be afraid to ask for help. It is better to be shown the right way to begin with than to risk losing your confidence.

EARLY LESSONS

Your first horse or pony at a riding school will obviously be well-used to many different people coming into his stable to lead him out for a lesson, but the basic rules always apply. His steadiness will give you confidence but you should not become over confident or casual. The same pony in a field at the beginning of spring may be an entirely different question.

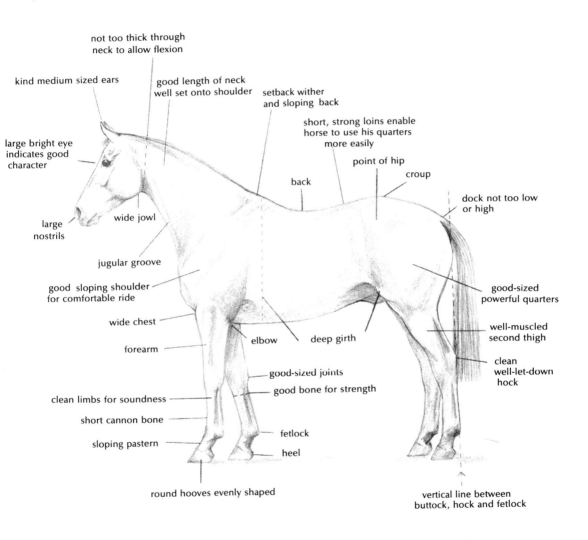

not too thick through
neck to allow flexion

kind medium sized ears

good length of neck
well set onto shoulder

setback wither
and sloping back

short, strong loins enable
horse to use his quarters
more easily

large bright eye
indicates good
character

point of hip

croup

back

dock not too low
or high

large
nostrils

wide jowl

jugular groove

good sloping shoulder
for comfortable ride

good-sized
powerful quarters

wide chest

well-muscled
second thigh

forearm

elbow

deep girth

good-sized joints

clean
well-let-down
hock

good bone for strength

clean limbs for soundness

short cannon bone

sloping pastern

fetlock

heel

round hooves evenly shaped

vertical line between
buttock, hock and fetlock

correct way to approach   incorrect way

Catching should never be a problem with well-handled ponies. Approach calmly towards the pony's shoulder keeping the headcollar close to you. A titbit may be offered or kept in the pocket until you have secured the headcollar. A noisy approach from behind the pony may cause him to run off in alarm and make catching difficult.

Catching *should* never be a problem with well-handled horses but small ponies especially can have completely different ideas to your own and it is usually best to have help if you think there may be problems. It is a good idea to *expect* everything of a horse or pony, familiar or unfamiliar, but it is equally unwise to *assume* anything.

Horses are creatures of habit, therefore the one caught up regularly at a set time every day will come more readily than the pony caught up just at weekends. As in the stable, always approach at the shoulder and talk to the pony as you approach. If the pony wears a headcollar in the field, you will only need to clip on the lead rope. Always have the clip-opening away from the pony's chin to avoid a pinch. If you have to fit a headcollar when catching, quietly slip the rope around the pony's neck, then pass the noseband over his nose and fasten the headstrap on the near (left) side.

Different people have different rules about titbits, but a few pony nuts or an apple produced from your pocket as a reward after catching is usually acceptable. Over-feeding of 'treats' such as mints can make a pony pushy or even prone to nipping, so it is as well to check with the owner before giving a pony anything extra.

The headcollar fixes on the near (left) side of the pony.

GETTING TO KNOW YOUR PONY

For your first few lessons your pony will probably be tacked up, waiting for you in his stable. Begin talking to the pony before you enter the box and, once in, close the door behind you. He may be tied up, with a headcollar over the bridle, or he may be standing loose in the box with the reins fastened out of the way to prevent them from getting tangled around his legs. Until you are familiar with tack fitting, it may be difficult to see how this has been done; sometimes the reins are looped around the neck and caught up in the throat lash of the bridle, or the reins will have been tucked back behind the stirrups. Safety is all important with horses, and the sensible stable owner/groom will tie up the saddled pony to prevent it from lying down and perhaps trying to roll with the saddle on.

Once in the stable, approach the shoulder, talking to the pony, and then pat or stroke his neck. Do not be afraid to get close to the pony – you cannot do everything at arm's length. Standing to the near side, untie the rope, and then, while still holding the rope, unfasten the headband of the headcollar and slip the noseband down over the nose. Horses and ponies that have been well handled respond to the command 'Over' if you need to move around them in the box. Do not move

A pony tacked up ready for a ride. He is tied securely with a quick-release knot and the reins are kept safely out of the way. Note the headcollar rope is fastened to a piece of string which would break in an emergency if the pony pulled back.

around the back of the horse – he can't see you – always pass in front, ducking under his neck if he is tied up.

Do not now leave the headcollar in a heap in the straw. Keep hold of the pony by taking the reins over his head and looping your arm through them, then hang up the headcollar by refastening the headband through the tying-up ring or hanging it up on a hook outside.

Before leading a pony out of a stable, make sure both stirrups are run up (i.e. they have not slipped down the leathers into the riding position, and therefore risk getting caught on the door as you go out), that the reins are not caught up in any other part of the bridle, and that the stable door is open to its fullest extent and not swinging shut as you walk out. Stand at the pony's left side with your right hand holding both reins together just behind his chin, and your left hand holding the reins further along nearer the buckle. If you are carrying a whip, hold this in your left hand.

When leading, you should walk at the pony's shoulder and he should walk forward to your command 'Walk on' and a slight forward nudge with your right hand. When coming out of the stable you need to be at the pony's head, so there is plenty of room for you both to pass through the door. Walk close to the pony and, if you need to turn him, do so by pushing his head away from you; you may experience your first sore toe if you do otherwise.

When dealing with an unfamiliar horse, always lead from the near side as this is usual, but if you eventually progress to owning, or even training, your own young pony, remember to familiarize him with being led from both sides. This will play a great part in helping the horse to move and work in a much more balanced way.

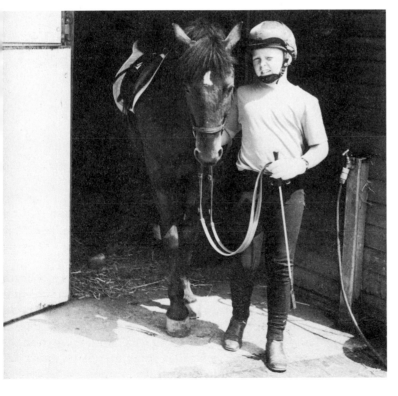

Leading a pony safely from the stable. The door is open wide and the stirrups are run up to prevent them from catching in the doorway. The handler stands behind the pony's head and pushes him forward.

The enjoyment of horses is just being around them, as much as actually riding. Being able to prepare a pony for riding helps familiarize the beginner with the pony and the basic saddlery used.

HEADCOLLAR

This should be made from leather and used as a basic measure of control for turning out in the field or tying up in the stable or yard. A headcollar has a noseband (which is sometimes adjustable) and an adjustable headband which fastens on the pony's near (left) side. The headcollar should fit comfortably. There should be about 2–3 finger-widths' space all round with the noseband resting about half way between the nostrils and cheek bones. The headband should sit comfortably behind the horse or pony's ears.

Standing level with the horse's head to his near side, the headcollar is removed by unfastening the headband and, with the rider holding both sides of the headcollar (the right hand passes underneath the horse's jaw), bringing it down over the nose.

ROPE

A lead rope with clip fastening is used with a headcollar. Make sure the clip faces away from the horse's chin. If he pulled back in panic when tied up, the clip could pinch his chin and cause a nasty wound.

When tying up, always tie the rope to a piece of string attached to the tie-ring, not directly onto the ring. Again, in an emergency, the string will snap releasing the horse and preventing injury.

A quick-release knot should always be used (*see* diagram). This can easily be untied by pulling the loose end. Always untie the rope before removing the headcollar and hold it over one arm. You may fasten the headcollar around the horse's neck before putting on the bridle. It is important to keep hold of the rope and not let it, the headcollar or the reins of the bridle dangle on the ground where they may tangle around the horse's legs and cause an accident.

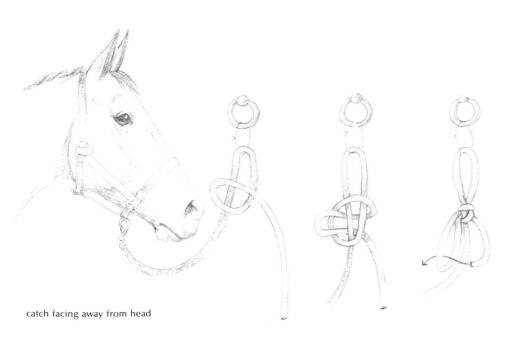

catch facing away from head

BRIDLE

The straps and buckles on the bridle can be confusing but only two need to be unfastened for fitting and removing.

To fit the bridle, stand level with the horse's head on his left side (pony on your right). Hold the bridle in the left hand and place the reins over the pony's head, so they rest on his neck. Grasp the bridle mid-way between the headband and bit. Hold it against the front of the pony's nose and with the same hand draw the pony's head in towards you. Use the other hand to support the bit and guide it into the pony's mouth.

With the bit in position, slide the headpiece back over the pony's ears and smooth the mane and forelock away from underneath it. Fasten the throatlash (2–3 finger-widths' space from jaw to strap) and noseband snugly.

To remove the bridle unfasten the noseband and throatlash. With the right hand, gently pull the bridle by the headband over the pony's ears, and hold the left hand under the mouth

A quick-release knot should always be used when tying up a pony.

Putting a bridle on. Note how the rider supports the bit as she encourages the pony to take it into his mouth. For safety's sake the pony remains tied.

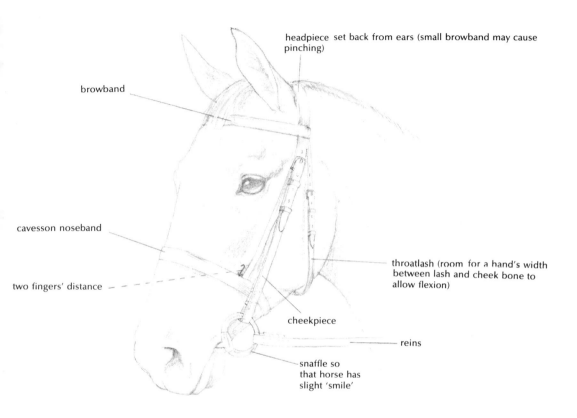

headpiece set back from ears (small browband may cause pinching)

browband

cavesson noseband

two fingers' distance

throatlash (room for a hand's width between lash and cheek bone to allow flexion)

cheekpiece

reins

snaffle so that horse has slight 'smile'

A correctly fitted snaffle bridle.

to support the bit when the pony releases it. Always wait for the pony to let go of the bit before removing the bridle or it may catch him in the teeth and frighten him. Refit the head-collar. Lastly, pass the reins back over the head and hang the bridle up neatly (reins looped up) before re-tying the pony.

SADDLE

Before fitting the saddle, replace the headcollar over the bridle and tie up. Make sure both stirrups are run up and the girth is resting over the seat of the saddle. Make sure the numnah (if used) is flat against the underneath of the saddle and well pulled up into the gullet. Lifting the saddle clear above the

When fitting a saddle, place it first high on the pony's withers then slide it back into the correct position. You will find it comes to a natural stop on the horse's back.

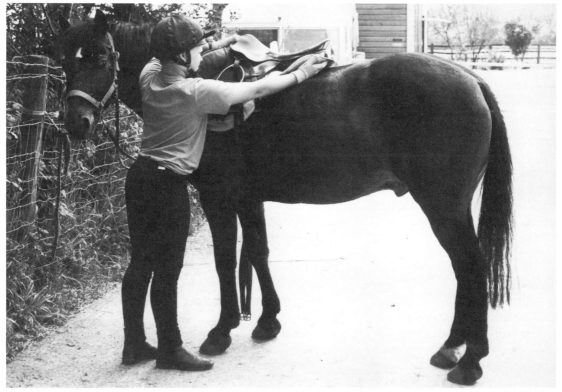

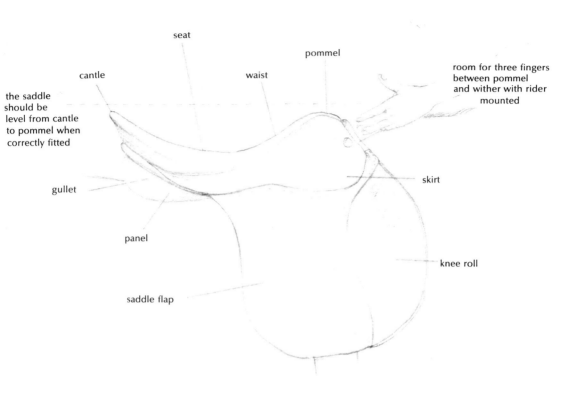

seat

pommel

cantle

waist

room for three fingers
between pommel
and wither with rider
mounted

the saddle
should be
level from cantle
to pommel when
correctly fitted

gullet

skirt

panel

knee roll

saddle flap

Points of the saddle.

pony's back, rest it gently down with the front of the saddle on the pony's withers. Now slip the saddle back a little until it comes to its natural resting place. Moving underneath the horse's neck, bring the girth down, then return to the off side to fasten the girth. Do not worry about making it tight at this stage – that can be done before mounting and re-checked after mounting.

PICKING OUT FEET

Before leading a pony out of a stable it is common practice in many riding schools to pick out the feet, thus preventing muck and straw from falling out onto a clean yard. With the pony tied up, pick up each foot in turn by running a hand down the back of the pony's lower leg, encouraging him to take his foot off

Picking out the feet is a fundamental part of horse management. It also prevents straw from being scattered over the yard if done before the pony leaves the stable.

the ground. Support the foot at the fetlock with one hand, and using a hoof pick, scrape out any muck from heel to toe, making sure you do not catch the tender heel or frog – clean down into the clefts of the frog. Collect the dirt into a skip to keep the stable clean.

Remember to put the headcollar up neatly and bring the reins over the pony's head before leading him out the stable.

Getting on a horse looks a fairly simple thing when watching an experienced rider, especially if he has the athletic ability to vault from the ground without the aid of a stirrup. As a beginner, you soon learn that a fair amount of spring is required in the thigh and calf muscles to set you lightly in the saddle.

It is usual before mounting to lead the pony away from his stable into a yard or enclosed riding manège. Near the stables there may be overhangs or low cables which could present a hazard to the rider on a bigger horse. Never, except under special circumstances, mount a horse or pony in the box; if you were to fall off you may be trodden on or, on riding out of the stable, you may catch your legs or head on the door. It is a good idea generally to use safety stirrups. These enable your foot to slip easily from the iron if you fall and thus prevent you from being dragged along the ground.

Until you become familiar with the mounting procedure it is better to have a helper to hold the pony's head. There are many things to remember, but do not let go of the reins as you get on; it is easily forgotten and without a helper the horse could walk forward, leaving you with one foot in the stirrup. To mount correctly, first take both reins into your left hand. Take up the slack in the reins sufficiently to prevent the horse from walking forward, and rest the left hand on the pommel of the saddle. Stand level with the girth and face the horse's tail. With your right hand, hold the stirrup leather just above the iron and twist it so that the back edge of the iron comes forward and the whole stirrup faces you. Keep the stirrup steady with your right hand while placing your left foot into it. You will find that you probably need to stand on tip-toe on your right leg and this will help to give you a bit more 'spring'. Now place your right hand over the top of the saddle so you are holding it roughly where the seat meets the flap on the off side. You are now ready to push yourself off the ground with the right foot, pivot your weight round in the left stirrup and swing your right leg clear over the horse's quarters, landing lightly with your seat in the saddle.

The problem when you are starting to ride is co-ordinating all the various actions into one fluent, swift movement. Mounting is obviously something you need to learn to do without hesitation. Horses should be schooled to stand still while being mounted, but for any number of reasons they may start to move forward and you will need to get aboard quickly.

Safety stirrups enable your foot to slip easily from the iron in the event of a fall, thus preventing you from being dragged along the ground.

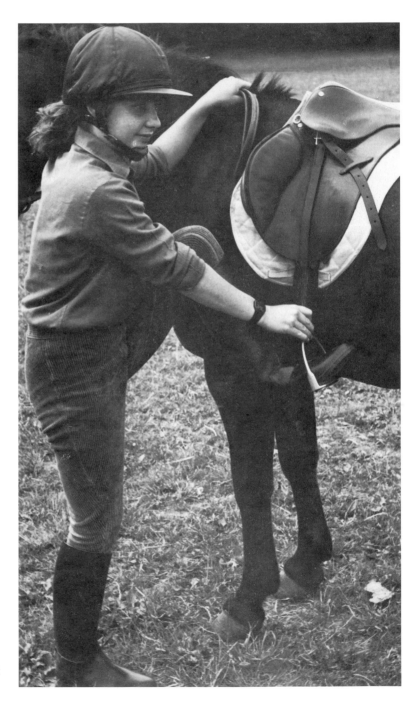

To mount correctly, face the pony's tail and place your left foot into the stirrup.

 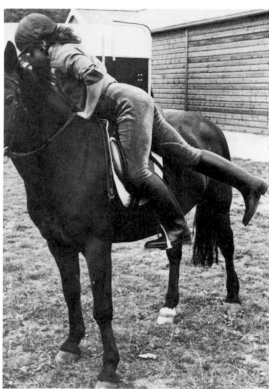

A SMOOTH START

Place your right hand across the seat of the saddle and spring up, landing lightly as you sit on the pony's back.

Let us run through the actions involved in mounting and mention the main difficulties again. Before doing anything else, check that the girth is tight and remember to keep hold of the reins. Second, keep the stirrup steady with your right hand. You may find it hard to reach the iron to begin with even if it has been adjusted approximately to your riding length. Lengthening the stirrup by a couple of holes will probably help. Next, as you spring up, try not to pull the saddle at the rear or cantle. This tends to twist the tree or frame of the saddle and should be avoided. Hold the seat on the opposite side or just rest your hand on the seat. As you pivot your left foot in the stirrup, try not to dig your horse in the ribs. Lastly, land in the saddle like a feather falling to the ground, not like a sack of potatoes. Once seated, place your right foot in the

Estimate the length of stirrup required by measuring the leather against your arm.

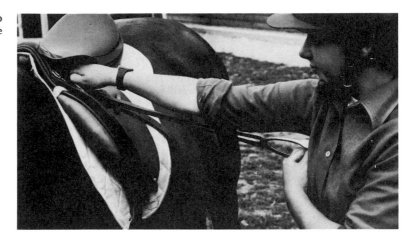

rub

A twisted stirrup leather feels uncomfortable under your leg and will make it sore if not corrected.

stirrup by turning the front edge of the iron round sideways and take the reins into both hands.

For safety's sake it is as well to have experienced help and an extra pair of hands to help you check and adjust the girth and stirrup lengths. Even though you may have tightened the girth before you mounted, you need to check it again once in the saddle, and possibly again once you have done a little work. Horses often blow themselves out when you first tighten the girth but after a while their waistlines return to normal.

DIFFERENT MOUNTING METHODS

If you are mounting a horse or pony which is a little too big for you, getting on from the ground may be very difficult and, especially while you are learning, it is better if you are given a 'leg up'. Holding the reins and the saddle as you would if mounting from the ground, but facing the side of the horse, stand on tip-toe on the right leg and bend the left leg up at the knee. Your helper will hold the shin of your left leg and, after you have counted to three, together, he will lift and you will spring at the same time, swinging your right leg over the horse's quarters.

Once you are practised at mounting from the more usual near side, learn and practise mounting from the off side. This is to help you and the horse, as to do the same exercise always from the same side builds up one set of muscles more than the

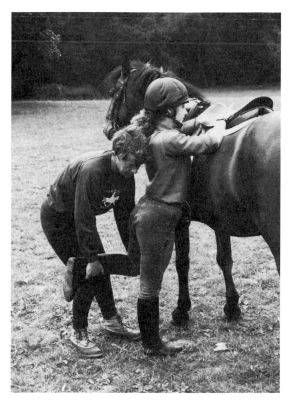

Getting on from the ground
may be difficult in the early
stages. A leg-up, shown here,
may be better.

Land lightly in the saddle and
place your right foot in the
stirrup.

other. From every point of view (including strain on saddlery),
mounting from a mounting block is far the best way as you can
step into the saddle rather than climb up into it. If you have to
get off while hacking in the countryside, you can usually find a
bank or a gate to help you remount, but of course there are
many times when you have to mount from the ground and it is
as well to learn it from the outset.

The quickest and most efficient way of all is by vaulting into
the saddle and it is as well to learn this while you are young and
supple. Holding the reins and saddle as if to mount normally
and facing the horse's side, the rider springs energetically with
both legs, first resting his tummy over the saddle, then swinging the right leg over the quarters and sitting upright.

Learning to ride on the lunge is rather like learning to drive with a qualified instructor who has control over the car in an emergency. Riding on the lunge is a little different in that the riding instructor has total control and you, the pupil, can become familiar with the seat and controls before having to steer, change gear and use the brakes yourself.

LUNGE EQUIPMENT

The horse is tacked up for riding normally, but extra equipment is used for lungeing. In addition to his bridle, the horse will also be wearing a lunge cavesson, which is a special type of headcollar with rings attached to the noseband. A long webbing rein is attached to the front ring and this is the contact the instructor has with the horse. The rein usually measures about

A horse tacked up ready for a lunge lesson.

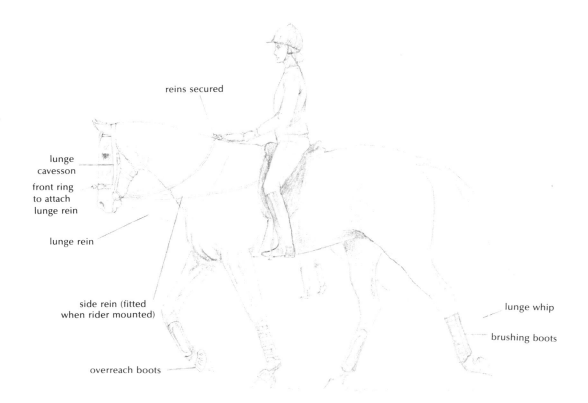

reins secured

lunge cavesson

front ring to attach lunge rein

lunge rein

side rein (fitted when rider mounted)

overreach boots

lunge whip

brushing boots

21ft (7m) and this measures the radius of the circle on which you ride, with the instructor in the middle. In addition, the instructor carries a long lunge whip which acts as the 'legs' and which, together with the voice, instructs the horse to make upward or downward transitions. The horse will also be wearing boots to protect his legs, especially from one leg knocking another.

THE LESSON

Usually at the start of a lunge lesson, the instructor will work the pony on each rein (in each direction around the circle) for a few minutes, in order to settle him down before helping you to mount. Once you are settled, the instructor will attach two reins, one each side of the pony between the girth straps and the bit. These side reins act as though the rider were holding the reins and give the pony a contact to work into.

In the earliest lessons the reins may be knotted, with a loop for you to hold, or you might hold the reins without actually shortening them and making any contact with the pony's mouth. The benefits for you are that you will become familiar with the movement of the pony and develop a balanced, relaxed seat before having to control him as well. The benefits for the pony are that his sensitive mouth is not pulled, nor his

(Above): A lunge lesson in progress. The instructor remains in control of the pony enabling the rider to concentrate on her position.

The correct way to hold a single snaffle rein. The thumbs should always be carried on top and the fingers kept closed but not tensed.

Lunge lessons will help develop a balanced independent seat. Always bear in mind the two straight lines: ear–shoulder–hip–heel and elbow–hand–horse's mouth as illustrated here.

sensitive back bumped as you learn the rising trot. When you are beginning you naturally want to get on to the next stage, but you will progress better and further if you learn the basics properly and thoroughly, rather than skipping through them.

As you progress, you will begin to take more control over the pony, learning the feel of transitions, the various paces, diagonals, and a square halt; but still always with the instructor at the other end of the lunge rein. When he feels you have sufficient control, you will be allowed 'off the lunge' and all the earlier lessons can begin to be used in actual practice.

Because both you and the pony work very hard during a lunge lesson, a session seldom lasts for longer than about twenty minutes, during which time you will change the rein every few minutes so that the pony works equally on both reins. These sessions often finish with some fun exercises like 'round the world in the saddle' when you turn around completely in the saddle, or touching various parts of the horse which the instructor calls out – all helping you to feel confident on the pony while at the same time improving balance.

Your lunge lesson may finish with some fun exercises like 'round the world in the saddle'.

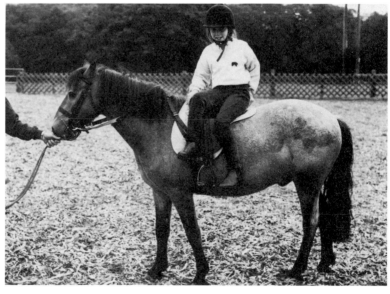

Very valuable lessons can be learned on the lunge and the most experienced riders at top-level competition still have trainers who lunge them in order to correct errors or habits which creep in.

A well-schooled horse and an experienced rider moving together in perfect harmony is a combination which takes many years to achieve. Regular tuition and patient practice added to a great deal of dedication are necessary, together with an ability to recognize that it may be you, and not the horse, at fault when things go wrong.

This lifetime's riding lesson begins when you mount a pony for the first time and are learning how it feels just to sit there, several feet above the ground. Early lessons may take two different forms, or a combination of them both. Most riding schools start beginner riders on the lunge, where the horse is controlled by the instructor who moves the horse around him on a large circle on a long rein. Other schools' early lessons will be on the leading rein, with the helper either on the ground or mounted.

The lungeing method enables the instructor to observe the actions of the rider, who can concentrate on his seat or position, before having to control the horse as well. This helps the rider to begin to develop an 'independent' seat, where the rider's body is in perfect balance with the horse at all times. The tendency for learner riders is to use the reins – which really means the horse's sensitive mouth – to balance themselves. The aim of work on the lunge is for the rider to develop sufficient control over his own body so that he carries himself on the horse instead of expecting the horse to do all the work.

RIDING POSITION

The classic riding position is really a very natural and basic one which, while the horse is standing still, is quite easy to achieve. The riding position can be practised on the ground, merely by placing the feet about 2ft (60cm) apart and bending the knees slightly. When mounted, your feet should remain directly underneath your hips. An instructor can help you achieve the correct position by 'placing' your legs for you against the pony's side. If you glance down, you should not be able to see your toes peeping out from underneath your knees. You should feel relaxed in your buttock and thigh muscles, not gripping in any way with the legs. A relaxed, deep position in the saddle feels most secure; unfortunately, the tendency when learning is to tense up, giving the same bouncy effect as

a pea on a drum. This becomes very uncomfortable for the horse and insecure for the rider.

When finding your position in the early days, you will hear an often-repeated reminder to help you to keep your body and legs in a straight, vertical line: 'ear–shoulder–hip–heel'. These are the points on the straight line, easily achieved at the halt but easily lost, even by more experienced riders, when the horse moves forward. The problem with losing the straight line is that you are immediately out of balance with the pony and your position is weakened. During early lessons on the lunge, you may find that holding a neck strap or the pommel of the saddle will help to prevent you from being 'left behind' (your upper body being jerked backwards while your legs slip forward) when the pony walks forward. At the walk, your instructor may ask you to do some exercises to help establish your position. Using the security of the saddle, pull up with the

Pulling up on the pommel helps you to relax your seat down into the saddle and establish a correct position. Note the straight line from ear through shoulder, hip and heel.

At all times try to keep 'with' the horse. Being 'left behind the movement' causes the lower leg to come forward, weakening the seat, while your hand may jerk the pony in the mouth.

hands while relaxing the seat and legs deep into the saddle. As you gain confidence, you can use just the outside hand (the hand on the outside of the circle you are on) on the pommel and allow the inside hand to relax down by your thigh.

CONFIDENCE IN THE SADDLE

Various exercises to help you feel more confident in the saddle can continue to be used as warm-up exercises when you are more experienced. Circling each arm, first holding it out at shoulder level, then up above the head and back to rest by your thigh, helps you to sit tall and straight when your arm is raised and deep and still when the arm is lowered. Such exercises also help to prevent you from stiffening up in your back and neck, which must remain supple. Your back is as much part of your 'seat' when it comes to effective riding as the part which actually sits in the saddle.

Once you are more secure, riding without stirrups helps to deepen your position in the saddle and allows the leg to 'grow' longer. Often, after a spell of riding without stirrups, you feel

Circling the arm helps to loosen the shoulder and prevents tension.

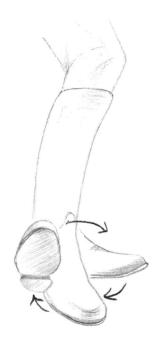

Circling the foot and ankle keeps the joint supple and helps you sink your weight into the heel.

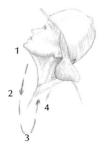

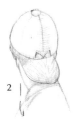

Circling the head helps loosen the neck and promotes flexibility. This should only be done at the halt in case of dizziness.

Shrugging the shoulders prevents tension building up in the neck and helps keep the shoulders down and relaxed.

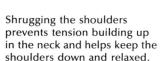

A rider under instruction on the lunge. The rider's lower outside leg has crept up and back, which is a common fault. Try to keep an equal weight on both seat bones.

you need to lengthen them when you replace your feet in the irons. The advantage of riding with a longer length is that the area of your leg in contact with the horse's side is increased and becomes more effective when the leg is used to encourage the horse to move forward.

When you first start to ride, a shorter length of stirrup gives a feeling of greater security. You can gain an approximate idea of the length you will require before mounting by checking the length of leather against the length of your arm. Holding one fist up by the stirrup bar, extend the leather and iron out with the other hand. The length you require is from your fist to your underarm.

When mounted, the broadest part of the foot rests in the stirrup iron, and you should allow your calf muscles to stretch and relax so that your heel stays level with, or drops a little below, the level of the toe. The toes should remain turned towards the front, although to turn them out momentarily does help to strengthen the depth in the heel. The flat area of ankle and the side of the lower leg stays in contact with the horse's side. It is fairly hard to encourage the calf muscles to stretch, as this is not a natural movement for the human leg, and even more experienced riders have to be constantly aware of the heel creeping up.

THE RIDER'S SEAT

After your first few rides, and almost certainly after riding without stirrups, you will discover what riders mean by their 'seat bones'. The bony framework around which our hips and buttocks hang is the pelvis. It is roughly bowl-shaped, supporting our insides and upper body and providing a structure to which our legs are attached. At the base of the pelvis, on each side, is a knobbly piece of bone called the ischial tuberosity, and, unfortunately for riders, it is these and the muscles surrounding them, which become sore when unaccustomed to

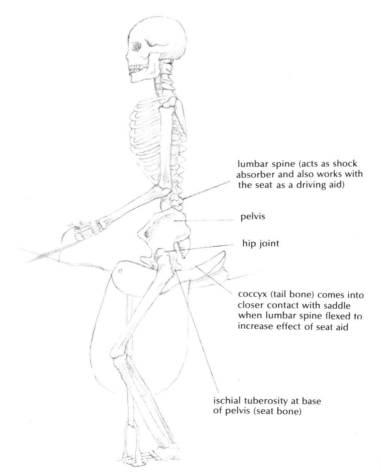

lumbar spine (acts as shock absorber and also works with the seat as a driving aid)

pelvis

hip joint

coccyx (tail bone) comes into closer contact with saddle when lumbar spine flexed to increase effect of seat aid

ischial tuberosity at base of pelvis (seat bone)

A skeleton rider showing the all-important pelvis and lower back.

riding. Fortunately though, the soreness soon wears off. The tail bone, or coccyx, makes a third point of contact between the skeleton and the saddle but you should avoid leaning back, or being left behind, so that your weight is taken off the seat bones. Experienced riders may sometimes appear to be leaning back, using all their 'driving' aids, but this is not necessarily correct according to teachers of classical riding.

SITTING STRAIGHT

A nervous, insecure seat causes the rider to tip forward onto the front of the pelvis. This may happen when you are tired or if your stirrups are too long.

Another problem often experienced by young or novice riders is a tendency to tip forward – you may hear the expression 'on

the fork'. Again, the weight is shifted off the seat bones and onto the front of the pelvis. This often happens when the rider is a little nervous or perhaps getting tired from unaccustomed exercise. If you tip forward, your legs usually slide back and this again weakens the seat making you less secure in the saddle. In some cases it may also be a signal for the horse to go faster, so if you are nervous it is a question of putting mind over matter and making yourself sit tall and relaxed! Riding with stirrups that are too long will also tip you forward so always make sure that the stirrups are of correct length and you are not reaching down for them.

Another very important part of the body to consider when sitting correctly is your head. If you consider that everything above your neck weighs 10–12lb, then if this is not held squarely over your shoulders it will put you off balance with the pony and make it more difficult for him to carry you. Always think about looking where you are going; on a lunge exercise or when schooling, get into the habit of looking about you. This makes it impossible to look down at the horse, a very common habit and fault, and also makes sure that you do not stiffen up in your neck. Good warm-up exercises include shrugging your shoulders up to your ears and letting them relax down again, or circling your head. Both help to keep your neck supple. Circling the head should only be done at the halt as you could become dizzy and lose balance. If you do not learn how to carry your head and neck at an early stage you may find that your neck and shoulders begin to ache after a riding lesson.

As important as your straight line, ear–shoulder–hip–heel, is another imaginary line viewed from the rear. This should run from the crown of your head, straight down your spine through the centre of the horse. Particularly when working on the lunge you will find that your weight is tipped, usually to the inside, and you are out of balance. As you gain experience you will become more aware of keeping an equal feel through both seat bones and will find it easier to sit square on the horse. Obviously, if you are riding with one stirrup longer than the other, this will make you slip to one side, so make sure someone checks your stirrup length until you can judge this for yourself. Not only is crookedness a fault, but it also places undue strain on both the rider's and the horse's backs.

During early lessons on the lunge, control over the horse is in the hands of the instructor but you will learn to hold your

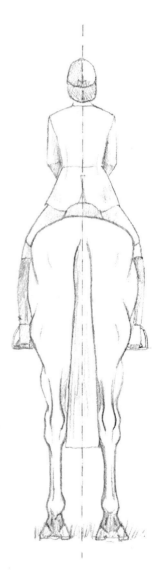

When viewed from the rear a straight line should bisect horse and rider from the crown of the rider's head through the centre of the horse.

arms and hands in the riding position and to hold the reins correctly. A good exercise is to stretch both arms horizontally in front of you at shoulder height, then drop them to your sides with elbows bent at 90 degrees, the forearms and wrists relaxed and the thumbs held uppermost. The upper arm should remain supple and straight. Think of it becoming part of your back and not breaking the straight line between shoulder and hip.

There is nothing in the classical riding position which requires stiffness or rigidity. Relaxation and suppleness can take a long time to achieve, but it comes a great deal easier if you can prevent bad habits from creeping in at the beginning.

Horse and rider – an independent seat enables a rider to stay in balance with his horse at all times.

The aids are the signals by which we communicate to the horse what it is we require of him. It is a sort of body language, in which the rider can use the influence of his own body to ask the horse to respond with his considerably larger frame. Experienced riders use precise, clear signals with young horses, asking for a little more response at each schooling session until the horse understands what is required. The experienced horse will then become as much a teacher for the novice rider as the instructor.

Riders refer to the 'natural aids' of:

Voice	Hands
Seat	Legs

VOICE

The voice is one of the first aids to which the young horse becomes accustomed, and horses can be schooled to respond to the voice only. It can be used to encourage, calm, reward, command and, if necessary, reprimand. This is all achieved by changing the tone of voice. At some more advanced stages of riding, in competition dressage for example, the use of the voice is forbidden, but at all other times it is a most valuable aid and helps the rapport between horse and rider.

When using the voice as a command, it is usual to raise the tone at the end of the word if you want the horse to move up a pace and trail the voice down for moving down a pace. For instance, ter-ROT to move from walk to trot, or TER-rot from canter to trot. 'Steady' and 'Whoa' also trail downwards, whereas 'Halt!' or 'Stand!' are definite one-syllable commands.

SEAT

The seat, really meaning the whole upper body, increases in influence with the experience of the rider until very subtle shifts of weight or musculature can be interpreted by the horse, particularly when performing such advanced movements as flying changes of leg or half-pass. Techniques such as these come only with years of experience, and cannot be achieved if a deep, relaxed, independent seat is not established at an early stage. The key is to rid the upper body, back and seat of all tightness and tension as these things can easily be transmitted to the horse. This is usually very difficult when

The horse should always be ridden forwards onto a contact with the bit. This horse has brought his head 'behind the vertical', possibly because the rider has failed to keep the energy coming through the quarters by allowing the lower leg to creep forward.

beginning, but can be greatly helped by having well-instructed lessons on a well-schooled horse.

It may help to think about carrying your upper body and head in a controlled but relaxed way, sinking your weight down equally into both seat bones – the lowest part of your pelvic girdle – keeping the thighs relaxed, and maintaining a straight line from your ear through the shoulder, hip and heel. Think about being a light weight for the horse to carry and avoid allowing the shoulders to slouch and your back to hunch. Practise the riding position by standing on the ground with your feet 2ft (60cm) apart and bending at the knees.

HANDS

The hands (and arms) should be carried free from tension from the shoulder, through the upper arm, forearm and wrist to the fingers. The rider has direct communication with the horse's sensitive mouth via the hands. Rigid hands might prevent a horse from moving forward properly and may set up resistances, for example – leaning on the bit, 'yawing' or opening the mouth to evade the bit, or snatching and dropping the bit – all things which break the communication between horse and rider. At all times there should be a constant positive feel in the hands as the horse seeks to take himself forward.

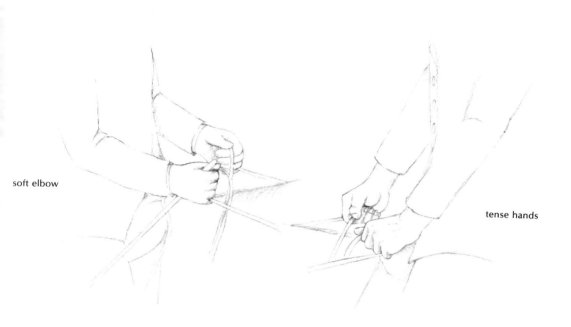

soft elbow

tense hands

When holding the reins the upper arm should remain supple and straight with a soft elbow, forearm and wrist. Tense, fixed hands restrict the horse's movement.

Rigid hands may prevent a pony from moving forward properly. Resistances may be set up such as leaning on the bit or opening the mouth to evade the action of the bit.

You should always remember to 'carry' your hands, keeping the elbow bent. Think of another straight line: elbow–hand–rein–horse's mouth. Keep the fingers closed around the reins but think of holding them as though you were holding two small birds; it will then be impossible to be tense in your arm.

Some bits are more severe than others but even the kindest bit is severe in hard hands. Always allow the horse to move forward, even when slowing down, alternately restraining and allowing with your hands.

LEGS

Effective riding is all about co-ordination. To the experienced rider, application of the aids becomes second nature.

Your legs are the 'driving' aid and control your pony's engine compartment – his hindquarters. The legs are effective when

the line, ear–shoulder–hip–heel, is maintained and the inside of the lower leg and ankle has greatest contact with the horse's side, just behind the girth. The well-schooled horse responds to a nudging vibration of the leg used out of the rhythm of the horse's movement. The horse will stop responding to the 'nagging' of a constantly banging leg. Sometimes you may actually have to kick as a short, sharp reminder and this is effective if you turn the toes out slightly, keep the heels down, and use the heel itself behind the girth.

Although you should not grip with the leg, you should maintain a consistent contact with the pony's side to make sure that he works correctly. Effective riding is all about co-ordination and no one aid is effective on its own – they must all work together. The seat and legs create energy from the horse's quarters and this is channelled through the horse's mouth and the rider's hands to help control the rhythm and speed of the movement. The legs and hands together are directional aids. The body and legs are used to shorten or lengthen a stride when used together with a more restraining or allowing hand. Asking a horse to move down through his paces should be achieved by straightening the back, closing the legs and gradually restraining and allowing with the hands. You are thus riding the horse forward all the time, even when asking him to halt.

ARTIFICIAL AIDS

Sometimes the rider's use of the natural aids needs further reinforcement and this is where careful use of the artificial aids can be made. The most common of these are the whip and the spurs.

Most riders learn how to carry and use a whip at an early stage and it is used to reinforce the leg if the horse is slow to respond. A long schooling whip is preferable as your hand does not have to be taken off the rein in order to apply it behind the girth.

Spurs, also used to give extra emphasis to the leg aids, should only be worn by more experienced riders as they must be used very carefully. They should always be blunt and the short length of them, not the ends, are used as extensions of the heel.

The great advantage of formal riding lessons on the lunge is that from the earliest moment you can begin to gain the all-important feel for what is going on underneath you. Even in the earliest lessons, when your basic position is being established without having to control the pony, or even hold the reins, you can begin to feel where the pony is placing his feet and whether his strides feel long or short. Later this will help you to know straight away if the pony is taking uneven strides – this may mean that he is lame. It is just one of the many observations you can begin to make which help you to recognize a happy, healthy horse from one that may be in some discomfort.

In order to build these impressions through the seat of your breeches, it is helpful to study the paces on paper so you know what to look for when mounted. To beginner and novice riders the walk often seems very boring and is neglected; this can make it difficult to produce a steady, active, attentive pace in which much useful work can be performed.

The walk is a four-time pace, which means that four evenly timed footfalls should be heard – and felt – to each complete stride. From halt, the horse moves first one hind foot forward, then the forefoot on the same side, followed by the hind and forefoot on the other side to complete the stride. To start with it is difficult to feel the hind legs moving and to know exactly what is happening. Look down briefly to watch the action of the left fore. When it comes forward you know that the left hind has just touched the ground. As the left fore touches the ground, the right hind is stepping forward and you may then glance at the right fore to see that moving. If you count 'two' as the left fore reaches the ground, and 'four' as the right fore

Sequence of steps in walk.

1   2   3   4

completes the stride, you can then begin to feel the complete four-time rhythm and put in 'one' and 'three' as you feel the hind legs stepping forward. This all takes some concentration, but you will soon be able to feel the steps without looking down.

POSITION AT THE WALK

The rider's position in walk should be the basic classical position with straight lines from ear–shoulder–hip–heel, and elbow–hand–rein–horse's mouth. Your body should be relaxed and supple and ready to follow the natural nodding movement of the horse's head. When you first hold the reins

These two pictures show the natural nod of the head in walk, which you should follow with your hands.

you will begin to learn how important it is to keep a constant, elastic contact with the horse's mouth and this should be kept, even though following the horse's movement. If you imagine the reins passing through a little ring on your elbows and being weighed down with a bag of sugar on each side, you will see that each time the horse nodded his head the bags of sugar would be lifted, but the contact on the reins would remain the same. So, although you must allow the hands to move forward as the horse nods down, they must move back again as his head rises, with no loss of contact.

Often the reins are thrown forward when asking the horse to walk from halt, but it is important to get the engine running first by shortening the reins, maintaining contact, sitting tall and quickly nudging with your legs until the horse responds and moves forward. As this happens, allow him to move but do not give the rein away or be tempted to tip forward in the saddle. The value of the basics established on the lunge will be very apparent once you are riding independently. If you are learning music, you cannot begin to play tunes until you can read the notes and, although you may feel that you want to get on and do more exciting things, unless you learn the basics thoroughly you will reach a stage where you will have to return to them in order to progress.

VARYING THE STRIDE

When you get more experienced you will learn to lengthen and shorten the stride in walk. There is no 'working' walk, as in trot and canter; the normal stride used in the school is medium walk, and advanced riders collect and extend the pace.

At the end of a lesson your instructor may tell you to encourage your pony gradually to take more rein, stretching his head and neck down towards the ground. This is known as a free walk and should continue with the same rhythm and relaxation of the previous work. It is one of the more difficult movements to perform well!

The trot is the most difficult pace for the beginner to master. The rhythm is two-time: for each complete stride, two foot falls are heard and the horse moves forward on alternate diagonal pairs of legs. This action produces a great deal of energy, not only forwards but upwards to some degree as well, as the horse bounces from one diagonal to the other. It is this upward energy that you must learn to absorb in your seat and back in much the same way as the shock absorbers on the wheels of cars prevent the passengers inside from having too rough a ride.

As I have already stressed it is most important to learn the basics of each pace while still on the lunge when you can secure your position by holding the pommel of the saddle or a neck strap. This helps the rider's seat to develop independently of the hands and, without such preparation, it is all too easy to use the horse's mouth, through the reins, to give a feeling of security.

When you trot for the first time it does feel very bouncy and your initial reaction may be to tip forward and raise the lower leg. This makes your position very insecure. However, the natural bounce of the pace forcing you out of the saddle actually helps to establish the beginning of rising trot. All early work with both young horses and beginner riders is performed in rising trot as this places less strain on the horse and is less tiring for the rider. This may not be apparent when you are first learning and the usual problem is that you try too hard!

Sequence of steps in trot.

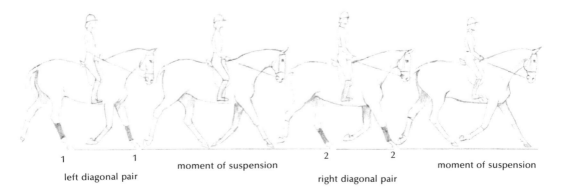

| 1 | 1 | moment of suspension | 2 | 2 | moment of suspension |

left diagonal pair   right diagonal pair

CORRECT RHYTHM

The first thing to establish is the actual rhythm of the pace. The instructor will suggest that you pull yourself down into the saddle and feel what is happening underneath. You will feel a definite one-two, one-two beat as first one hind leg and the opposite foreleg touch the ground, and then the other pair or diagonal do the same thing. There is a moment's suspension when all four legs are off the ground. The art of rising trot is simply to allow each alternate beat to nudge you slightly upwards and forwards out of the saddle. People often think they have to stand up in the stirrups to rise, and then not only do they get the rhythm wrong, but they also come much too far out of the saddle. Your leg position should not alter from that in the walk and the upper body inclines slightly forward. As the pony bounces you up, straighten the knees slightly and slide the seat forward a little, just raising the buttocks out of the saddle. It is not necessary, and is incorrect, to haul yourself out of the saddle, or to grip with the knees. If you rise on beat one, just relax the legs again and sit back in the saddle for beat two. Quite a degree of muscular control and co-ordination is demanded and you will probably find that you miss quite a few

In rising trot the rider takes a slightly more forward position.

beats in the early lessons, but do not be discouraged. You will see how necessary it is to have your own body under control before you have to control the horse as well.

In rising not too far out of the saddle it is important to be aware of how you return to the saddle after each alternate bounce. Remember that your pony is a living creature with a sensitive back and you should sit softly in the saddle, avoiding bumps and jars which may make him sore. It might take a few lessons to get it right and you may find it tiring but to carry on incorrectly could strain your own back as well.

DIAGONALS

The term 'diagonal' has often been used and early lessons on the lunge will help you to recognize on which diagonal pair of legs the horse is advancing. In rising trot, a rider is said to be sitting either on the left or the right diagonal and this becomes more important as work in the school proceeds. If working on a left-handed circle, or on the left rein, it is usual to sit on the right diagonal, which is as the right foreleg and left hind leg reach the ground. If you are on the right rein, you should sit on the left diagonal, which is as the left foreleg and right hind reach the ground. When learning which diagonal you are sitting on, it is helpful to glance down at the outside shoulder

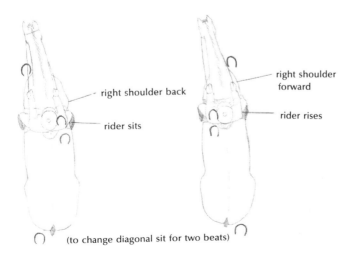

right shoulder back

rider sits

right shoulder forward

rider rises

(to change diagonal sit for two beats)

Trotting on the right diagonal.

(this normally means the one nearest to the outside of the circle or school) and watch as it comes back. If you are sitting as it comes back you are on the correct diagonal. If you are rising as it comes back, you are incorrect and need to change by sitting for an extra beat. Eventually you should easily be able to tell which diagonal you are on.

When you are more experienced and are hacking out in the countryside, do not forget to change the diagonal at regular intervals as this helps to keep the horse's musculature more balanced.

AIDS TO TROT

The aids for moving forward from walk to trot are similar to those from halt to walk. You should shorten the reins, sit tall and use quick nudges with the legs to encourage the pony to step forward into trot. Be ready to stay with the pony as he moves forward, and do not get left behind.

Once in trot, you should stay sitting for a few strides in order to establish the pace and then you should commence rising on the correct diagonal. Your leg aid must be maintained to keep the pony going forward and you will probably find it easier to give a couple of quick nudges each time you sit back in the saddle.

When your rising trot is fairly well established you may find it easier to spend longer periods in sitting trot. This puts quite a different strain on your abdominal muscles and you may find it tiring or get a 'stitch'. Do not be afraid to tell your instructor and have a rest, or go into a rising trot. Good abdominal muscles actually help your back, which is acting as a shock absorber all the time, and if you can think about pulling your abdomen *up*, lifting your rib cage and relaxing the shoulders you will find you are able to sit to the trot much more comfortably.

To make the downward transition from trot to walk, you should resume sitting trot if you have been rising, sit tall and push the pony forward with the legs into an alternately restraining and allowing hand. It is important that the pony continues to move forward and does not drop back into a slow walk, so the leg aid should be maintained to encourage him to walk forward smartly.

VARYING THE STRIDE

As a beginner and novice, most of your trot work will be performed in normal 'working' trot, which is the basic pace for all school work. However, when you get a little more advanced you will learn to ask for a slightly longer stride by applying a stronger leg and allowing a little more with the hand. You will be asking the horse to step further underneath himself and to generate more energy with his hind legs so that each complete stride covers more ground than the working pace. It is important to establish the rhythm of the trot-one-two, one-two, as this should remain unaltered and the pace should not quicken. At much more advanced levels these lengthened strides progress into the medium and then the extended trot where the horse steps forward to his maximum and appears to float over the ground. Again at advanced levels, the working stride can be shortened to 'collect' the trot. Once more, the rhythm stays the same but the pace becomes more elevated and the moment when all four feet are off the ground becomes slightly longer. In advanced dressage this is taken even further in the movements of passage – a highly collected trot, and piaffe where the horse trots on the spot which is one of the ultimate achievements in riding.

The rider must remain very supple to absorb the energy of a medium or extended trot. This rider should be a little more relaxed in her lower leg. A really independent seat is needed to sit to these advanced paces.

When you are learning, the canter seems a big stage up and to many it seems like a much faster pace. In fact, the canter need not cover any more ground per stride than the trot and it is a much easier pace to ride, being a rocking horse action rather than a bounce. Depending to some extent on the pony you are riding, the canter is therefore rather more comfortable. It was in fact the pace chosen by pilgrims of the Middle Ages as they made their way to Canterbury. The word 'canter' is derived from the 'Canterbury gallop', being the three-time pace which was more comfortable for the rider and less jarring on the horse's legs.

The three-time rhythm of the canter means that there are three footfalls for each stride. Riders talk about the left or right leg 'leading' in the canter, the leading leg being the third step of the stride made by either the left or right foreleg. In left canter, the horse steps forward first with his right hind, then the left hind and right fore together as a diagonal pair, and lastly the left fore followed by a moment with all four legs off the ground before the right hind steps forward again. For right canter, the left hind steps forward, then the right hind and left fore, followed by the right foreleg and a moment of suspension.

The canter is an easier pace to ride than trot, providing you keep a relaxed position in the saddle.

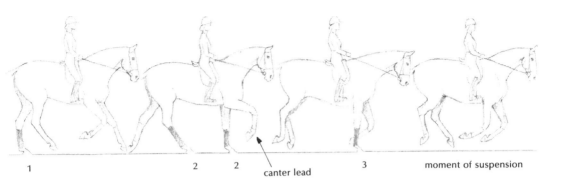

1   2   2   canter lead   3   moment of suspension

PREPARING TO CANTER

Sequence of steps in canter.

Sometimes riders experience difficulty when asking the horse to move forward to canter and often this is because of over-anxiety. It is important to remember to keep the trot steady and balanced before asking for canter, and not to push the horse into a faster unbalanced trot from which he will not make the upward transition successfully. When learning, or

It is easy to become anxious when asking for canter. Keep sitting tall, and looking up when applying the canter aid.

It is easier to ask for canter on a circle or coming through a corner.

when riding novice horses, it is easier to ask for canter on a circle or coming through a corner. If you keep calm, it happens much more easily. Concentrate on riding the corner or circle accurately, steadily and in balance, in sitting trot. Use the inside leg to make sure the pony is going forward and that his hind legs are placed well underneath him. The reins should be shortened a little to prepare the horse. The inside rein is directional to guide the horse around the corner and the outside rein contains the forward energy. Your instructor may refer to this as riding with the 'inside leg to the outside hand'. If the energy is not there, the pony will not be able to step forward into canter, in rather the same way that a car driver might change into a higher gear before the engine has picked up enough speed. When dealing with horses it is important not to confuse energy with speed, and to contain the energy in the hand rather than letting it escape in a faster and faster trot.

With your pony positioned correctly around your inside leg all you need to do is bring the outside leg a little further back on the pony's side and apply a little pressure. This encourages the outside hind leg to make the first step forward into the canter stride. Remember that the 'outside' is the outside of the bend of the pony, which is usually the side nearest to the edge of the school or arena. Therefore, on the left rein, the outside leg is the right one. If the first step in canter is the right hind, the left hind/right fore diagonal will follow and finally the left fore which is the correct leading leg.

Once in canter, you should sit tall, allowing your seat to relax into the saddle, and your hips to follow through the rocking motion of the stride. Your outside leg should remain a little further back than normal, brushing against the pony's side to remind him to keep taking canter steps forward, rather than breaking back into trot. The inside leg should keep the energy going by giving quick nudges out of rhythm with the stride.

PROBLEMS WITH THE CANTER

When you are learning, there can be a tendency to tip forward when asking for canter but this weakens your position and may send your pony out of balance. There are some occasions when it might be correct to lean forward, but if you are learning on a well-schooled pony you should stick to the classical position and aids for canter.

It is unlikely that, as a beginner, your lunge lessons will include any canter work as it is difficult to keep the correct balance and only more experienced riders have the necessary co-ordination. For this reason you will be unable to get a feel of the pace before you yourself have control over the pony and have to co-ordinate all your own efforts into asking him for the upward transition. If you have been asked to try for canter between two given markers in the school, try to keep calm and relaxed, preparing your pony in the way described. If things go wrong and the pony does not canter, do not keep trying if you have come out of the corner and are riding in a straight line. If

There is a tendency for beginners to tip forward when asking for canter and thus losing the contact. This tends to push the pony into a fast unbalanced trot.

the pony merely quickens the trot, give up all attempts to canter until you have restored a correct rhythm, and regained balance and control. You can then ask again in the next corner. If you are in a class the instructor will probably ask each leading rider in turn to go forward to canter in the next corner and then canter a circle at the free end of the school (away from the others who are probably walking around). Even in this situation, if your pony does not canter when you first ask, you can use the circle to ask again. If you can keep your head and do not get flustered you will achieve much more.

As you become a little more experienced you will learn different school movements that help the upward transition to canter – they help to establish the correct bend in the horse, around the inside leg into the outside hand. In all movements, however, you must concentrate first on making sure that your pony is moving forward energetically in a controlled manner. You may try riding a circle smaller than the standard one and then push the pony out onto a bigger circle again, not by directing him out, but by pushing him slightly sideways and outwards while still travelling forward on the circle. If you are containing the outward movement in the outside hand and preventing the quarters from swinging out by bringing the outside leg further back than normal position, you will see that it will take only a nudge of the outside leg to ask for canter.

If you are riding 'large', or around the outside of a schooling area, as you ride the corner you can try to bring the pony's forehand just a little off the track and then apply the canter aid; again, the object of the exercise is making sure that you have a good contact in the outside hand.

Sometimes horses strike off on the wrong leg – that is leading with the right leg on the left rein or vice versa. Experience will teach you to recognize when you are on the wrong lead and when this happens you should return to sitting trot, re-balance your pony and ask for canter again, making sure your aids are clear.

If your pony canters to command but you do not keep sufficient energy coming through from behind, he may either fall into trot or canter in four-time rhythm, which is incorrect. Again, it is probably better to trot, re-balance and ask for a more energetic canter next time. You will only begin to recognize the irregularities of the pace as you gain in experience and until then it is very important to have an instructor or knowledgeable helper on the ground to tell you when things are going wrong.

Like the trot, at advanced levels the canter stride can be lengthened to a medium and extended canter, or shortened to a collected canter. In all cases a constant rhythm should be maintained throughout.

A transition is the name given to moving up or down from one pace to another. Riders always talk about moving 'forward', whether the transition is upwards (from walk to trot or trot to canter), or downwards (from canter to trot or trot to walk). It means that the rider should be creating sufficient controlled energy for the horse to be able to step actively into his next pace. It is easier to understand in upward transitions, when each successive pace requires more effort from the horse, than when making downward transitions. However, unless the horse is working actively with his hind legs to generate energy, he will 'fall' or move lazily into the next pace and continue to idle along in that pace. This is very often the case when moving forward to walk from trot – if the rider is not working properly, the horse will take a rest too.

For a horse to be truly moving forward, he should be 'tracking up' which means that the hind feet are coming far enough forward to step into the tracks left by the forefeet, or even a little in front of them.

The basic aids for all upward and downward transitions remain the same, with only slight alterations of leg position. Your first job is to make sure you have your pony's attention, and check that he is really moving forward actively into your outside hand, with the inside leg nudging against his side. This preparation can usefully take the form of a 'half-halt' – taking a momentary check of the forward movement on the outside rein but immediately allowing again with the hand and nudging with the inside leg to send the pony on.

When moving up a pace, you should shorten the reins a little and sit tall. Your hands should not restrict the pony in any way and you should remain relaxed through the shoulders, arms and wrists. Your legs, back and seat should then work together to send the pony forward, although while learning you will probably feel it is your legs which are doing most of the work, especially if your mount lacks schooling.

MAKING GOOD TRANSITIONS

Transitions should not be sudden or jerky, but flow upwards or downwards. Early work on the lunge will establish a secure basic seat which enables you to maintain your position throughout the transition without tipping forward or being left

Follow the three pictures and see how the pony moves from trot to walk. The near side hind leg in the second picture comes forward to make the first walk step in the third.

behind the movement. This is most likely to happen if you are in a class lesson and your pony plays 'follow my leader', rather than waiting for your command. No matter what the pony in front of you has done, it is important that you remain in total control of yours and apply the aids correctly, keeping at least one or two horses' lengths between you and the pony in front. This is especially important when making downward transitions rather than using another pony as a set of buffers to stop you.

UPWARD TRANSITIONS

As the pony steps forward into the new pace, you should allow sufficiently with the hands so that you do not immediately block the movement, thus making him stop again. At the same time, your legs should continue to work to keep the energy coming through from behind. It takes some time for the novice rider to learn the feel of the pony's hindquarter activity, but it is most important that this is combined with a relaxed, swinging back and rounded topline. Any problems you may have yourself with stiffness or rigid hands will set up resistances in the pony and make your transitions untidy. The most common problem is that of causing the pony to raise his head and become hollow in the back, usually because of restrictions in the hands. This makes it impossible for the horse to place his hind legs correctly underneath him and the energy or activity of the pace is lost.

In upward transitions, hollowing may occur because there is not enough energy to begin with. If you have a problem creating sufficient activity to make good transitions, work on a circle helps as it is easier to keep the pony rounded and active between the inside leg and outside hand.

DOWNWARD TRANSITIONS

In downward transitions, where the pace is decreased by pushing forward with the legs into a more restraining hand, you should take care that you do not begin to pull back on the reins. The feeling you should have is one of the pony taking you forward, not of you pulling him back.

You may sometimes hear riders refer to direct and indirect transitions. When learning, all transitions are progressive in that if you are asked to canter from walk you will ask for a few preparatory steps in trot first. This is an indirect transition from walk to canter. Advanced riders will make direct transitions from halt to canter, canter to walk and so on, requiring very precise aids and lots of activity in all paces to be able to spring readily from one to another.

The rider here has fixed her hands in asking for the downward transition from canter and has caused the horse to raise his head and hollow in resistance.

The purpose of school work is to produce a competent rider and the exercises performed will teach you the basic methods of communication so that you have full control of your horse.

It is important for you as a novice that your lessons are varied, busy and interesting. There are two problems in the ordinary riding school situation. First, in a class lesson of six, each individual will receive only ten minutes' tuition in an hour and, second, it is very often the least experienced instructor who teaches the least experienced riders. If you know and appreciate what you are striving for, you can keep working towards this, even when attention is not fixed on you. In any case, it really is worth while from time to time to have a lesson on your own, or shared with one other person, when there is more time to discuss and work out problems.

LAYOUT

Standard 60×120ft (20×40m) manège showing the area covered by 10, 15 and 20m circles and the route for a 3-loop serpentine.

You will notice that all formally laid out schools are marked with various letters. These act as a grid on a map and all

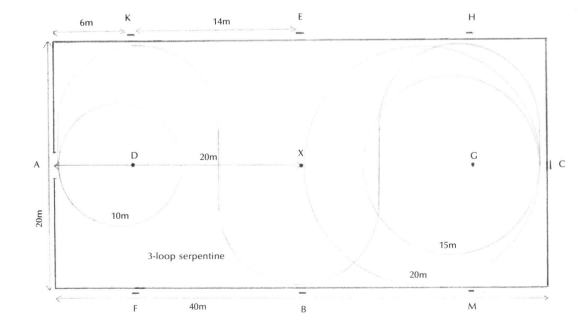

exercises and movements within the school are performed in areas specified by reference to one or more markers. Clockwise around the school they are A, K, E, H, C, M, B and F (you could remember All Kind Equines Help Children Make Better Friends), with X as the centre marker. Standard schools measure 60×120ft (20×40m) so the markers conveniently slice it up. A circle with a diameter A–X will be referred to as a 20-metre circle and you will find much of your early work is based on this figure. This may sound easy but the problem for many riders (not just beginners) is that 20-metre circles become rather egg-shaped. Ponies fall in around their corners or drift out towards the track (the outside path around the arena). To prevent these things you must be in control, with your legs and hands co-ordinating to keep the pony moving forward actively and in balance. In fact the pony must be kept 'straight' even though he is being asked to turn – this means that a line drawn from between the pony's ears to the top of his tail should be the same line as you are riding around the circle. Your inside leg nudges the pony's side to keep him moving and to keep him out on the circle; your outside leg stays back behind the girth to prevent his quarters from swinging out. Your outside hand allows sufficiently for the pony to move his forehand around on the circle, and controls the forward movement, while the inside hand softly indicates direction. You, the rider, should be sitting up and looking in the direction you wish to travel. This as much as anything else will help you ride to an accurate circle.

Ride every movement as accurately as you can; on a circle the mid-line of the horse follows the bend.

TURNS AND CIRCLES

Turns and circles form an important part of school work as it is easier to achieve greater activity from the horse's quarters. When you move from a circle or turn to a straight line the activity can be lost, so you should always think of a corner or circle as an opportunity to prepare for the straight line. Build up a little energy in reserve, perhaps by making one or two half-halts, and then, on starting the straight line, contain the energy in the outside hand which will keep the horse straight. When riding down the long side of the school this may seem easy but more accuracy is called for if you are asked to turn down the centre or three-quarter line when the pony may drift

The half pirouette is a good straightening and suppling exercise. This pony has rather too much bend in his neck as the rider asks him to move his forehand around his quarters. The rider should keep a better contact in the outside (left) hand as she asks the pony to move to the right.

off course. If you get used to riding accurate, energy-building corners, you will find it easier to ask for upward transitions or some lengthened strides as you will have learned how to gain the horse's attention and have him really working for you.

CREATING ENERGY

While you are having to think about all these things – the energy, straightness and what your hands and legs should or should not be doing – do not forget to try to fix a sense of rhythm in your mind. If the activity you have created is allowed to run away, the horse will be sent out of balance. This is especially important when asking for upward or downward transitions, or indeed when you progress to jumping lessons. Think of the horse as being a spring held between your fingers.

A good example of how a circle should be ridden. The horse remains straight on the circle as the rider keeps the contact in the outside hand.

You can make it bouncier or less so depending on the pressure you use, but if you let go at one end you lose all the bounciness or energy you have created. So your legs create energy to be controlled by the hands.

Concentrate on riding each movement as accurately as you can; feel that you are actually *riding* rather than being a passenger on a push button pony who performs all school movements on automatic pilot. Use every opportunity to learn to feel what is happening beneath you – the sequence of the footfalls at walk, trot and canter, whether you are sitting on the correct diagonal at the trot, whether the pony has struck off on the correct leg at canter or whether the pony is standing squarely at halt (without looking down to check!).

Providing you have a good instructor there is no need ever to feel bored by work in the school. The good teacher will pass on his own enthusiasm to his pupils.

Learning to jump seems a major milestone in a rider's progress. In fact it is a progression of flat work, and not something separate at all. Correct preparation on the flat is essential for successful jumping and jumping itself can improve and vary flat work.

A GOOD APPROACH

The exhilaration of jumping makes it much more exciting for many riders than dressage work, but your riding instructor will need to be confident that your ability on the flat is sufficient for you to begin to learn to jump. A basically secure, independent seat is necessary if you are to help rather than hinder a horse to jump. You should have control over your own balance and not expect to have to hang onto the reins like a lifeline. The pony must have the freedom of his head and neck when he jumps in

Using poles around a circle helps to encourage a pony to engage, or use to best effect, his hocks and activate his quarters to maximum benefit.

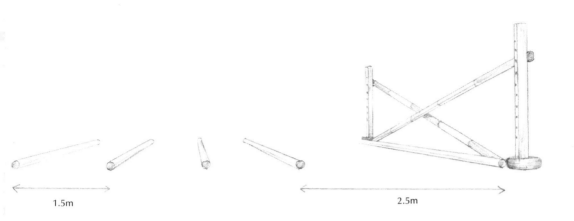

1.5m   2.5m

order to balance himself and the control you have over your own body should enable you to remain in balance.

Learning to jump begins with the early work on the lunge but you will really feel you are getting somewhere when lessons begin to take in work over a few ground poles. Usually about four to six poles are placed in a straight line approximately 4ft (1.2m) apart. You will be asked to turn off the track, to make a straight approach towards the poles, and continue to trot over them, almost as though they were not there. The distances between the poles should be such that the horse trots over them in his stride without having to make any extra effort. The rider's task is to make sure that a good turn is made into the approach (by looking at the poles before actually making the turn) and then maintaining an active, rhythmic trot throughout the exercise. You should continue to look ahead of the poles, to the point in the school where you will turn back onto the track.

When you have shown that you can complete this type of exercise, knotting the reins and holding your arms out to your sides while trotting over the poles will help to further develop your ability to stay in balance with the pony and then, with stirrups shortened, you may negotiate the whole line in forward, jumping position, with or without the reins. If you feel yourself losing balance, hold a section of mane or the front of the saddle for security, but do not grab at the reins, because by doing so you will pull on the pony's mouth, interfere with his forward movement and therefore upset his balance and rhythm.

A basic line of trotting poles with a double space allowed between the last pole and the fence to allow the horse to take one trot stride.

This pony shows a good active trot over the poles. The rider allows with her hands while maintaining her position in rising trot.

When a horse jumps successfully it is not the actual jump he makes but the way in which he has been prepared and ridden into the fence that is important. Early pole work requires just as much preparation and makes the introduction of a small fence no more difficult than jumping poles.

FROM POLES TO JUMPS

When you are ready for this stage, the instructor will remove the second last pole in the line and make a small fence at the end. (The way in which you ride the exercise is exactly the same except that it is probably better to ride in sitting trot as you approach and take up jumping position for the poles themselves.) This helps to ensure that you are allowing sufficient

Jumping a small course is the next stage from basic pole work. Here a young rider and her pony show how it should be done. Always look up and ahead while jumping and allow the pony freedom of his head and neck.

rein for the pony to stretch his head and neck forward and down.

A second fence might then be introduced, in which case the horse may naturally canter after the first and over the second jump. This is perfectly normal as the jump is merely a phase of a canter or gallop stride for the horse, and he therefore finds it much easier to jump from this pace than from trot. Do not be tempted to look into the bottom of fences, or look down as you jump. Always look up and ahead in the direction you wish to go.

The basic rules applied to general school work – controlled activity or energy, straightness, rhythm and balance – remain the same for jumping, at whatever level, with the added rule that you should do all in your power to allow the jump itself to be as unrestricted as possible.

DO prepare correctly on the flat; make a good approach; look where you are going; and keep an active, rhythmic trot.

DON'T interfere with your pony's mouth; look down; restrict your pony's head and neck; or look into the bottom of fences.

At the very early stages of your riding career you will be very concerned with training yourself. A great deal of concentration is required in co-ordinating the aids, listening to instructions and just making sure the horse is doing what you are asking of him.

RIDING NATURALLY

Gradually, your own actions will become more natural and spontaneous and you can then really feel able to start to learn what is happening under the saddle. An appreciation of the sequence of hoofbeats at each pace, correct diagonals and canter leads will have been learned in early lessons. Under continued tuition your riding will become more effective. The driving aid which you might previously have thought meant

Ineffective driving aids. A weak seat and legs allow the horse to fall onto his forehand.

icking with your legs, should mean pressure with the legs or
ubtle use of the seat and back on well-schooled horses or
onies. As your seat is the point of contact with the pony, you
egin to appreciate how effective your driving aids are; do the
ind legs move actively forward and does the pony's back feel
elaxed and 'swinging' underneath you?

The feel of the pony's mouth through your hands is another
kill which develops with practice. Rein contact should remain
ven and constant, neither giving too much so that the reins
lacken, nor pulling back. When you can ride the horse
ctively forward in balance and rhythm, he will naturally seek
his contact and give you the feeling that he is taking you
orward. If, while you are riding, you feel one arm or shoulder
ets tired more quickly, it may be that the pony is holding the
it to one side of his mouth and tilting his head. He may snatch
t the bit, continually bringing his nose back into his chest in
n attempt to drop the bit. Such evasions may be because of
hysical problems in the horse himself, the rider's one-
idedness, or his lack of skill. A correct diagnosis can be given
y an instructor on the ground or a more experienced rider
vhose skills are more complete.

The horse may tilt his head to
one side if he is stiff in his body
or if he has painful teeth.

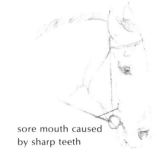

sore mouth caused
by sharp teeth

Sharp teeth in need of rasping
may cause a pony to avoid
taking a true contact with the
bit.

If the pony continually puts his head up you may not be riding him forward energetically enough, or he may have a weak conformation which prevents him from lowering his head and neck. If the feeling you experience in your hands is very dead and heavy, your back and seat may be dead and heavy too, pushing the pony onto his forehand.

Your in-built sense of rhythm should be developed so you can regulate the rhythm of the pace (by using different pressure of your seat), and also judge the steps within the pace. If there is irregularity here, the horse may be 'unlevel' or be taking uneven steps, possibly because of the unbalanced development of his muscles. He may actually be lame and it is obviously essential that a rider can recognize such problems.

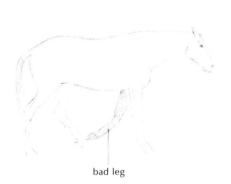

bad leg

shortened stride

A lame horse nods his head as the sound leg touches the ground.

Some observations can be made only if you first know what is normal for a particular horse or pony and hopefully you will have the opportunity to build a relationship with an individual mount. When you know what is usual you will soon recognize when something is wrong. If a normally energetic horse appears slow and depressed, he may be ill and running a temperature. If a normally placid horse becomes full of himself he may have been given too much food.

CARE AFTER RIDING

After a riding session, your first consideration should be for the care of the horse. After the tack has been removed the chief concern should be that the horse has suffered no injury during the lesson or ride, such as knocking one leg with another, picking up a thorn or sustaining any other wound. This means cleaning and checking the legs and picking out the feet. If the horse is muddy from a hack, a thorough rinse with cold water cleans the legs and feet and makes examination much easier, although care should be taken to dry the heels well. The next concern is to make sure that the horse will come to no harm following the ride. If he is stabled there should be enough bedding to prevent injury if he decides to roll. The headcollar, rope and any other saddlery should be removed

This horse is not working correctly from his quarters through to his forehand. Note how inactive his hind legs seem. His tail is swishing in resistance and he appears lazy.

Care of the horse after riding is very important. If the horse is sweating or warm after work an anti-sweat sheet is fitted, always with a surcingle or roller. The rider here is washing the legs with cold water from a hosepipe. Make sure the heels are properly dried after washing to prevent cracking.

from the box. If the horse is still warm, consider whether to replace rugs or fit an anti-sweat sheet, either of which should be correctly secured with a roller. Clean water should be available at all times.

If the horse has to be used again soon afterwards in a riding school situation, the tack may be left on but the girth should be slackened and the reins fastened up out of the way. The horse should be tied up in a box and a rug or sweat sheet thrown over his back if the weather is cold or the horse hot.

In observing these basic rules you begin to extend your knowledge of horse management, and riding becomes a much more complete sport when you further your interest to the care of the horse.

Once you are competent enough, hacking out into the countryside will provide an extra exciting element to your riding during which you will continue to learn outside a formal lesson situation.

As ever, safety is the watchword and you should never ride out on a horse or pony that is beyond your capabilities. Horses often get excited when out, especially when in the company of others, and they can also get 'spooked' by rubbish in hedgerows or pheasants suddenly fluttering up under their feet. Your pony can become quite different to ride from the animal you may be used to in the school, and unless you have the skills to manage him, you present a potential danger to yourself and other countryside users. It is important that you should feel confident (but not over-confident) about hacking out. Horses sense anxiety and if you tense up in fear the horse,

Horses and ponies are always keener when out in the countryside. You should be sure your skills are equal to the task.

too, becomes more agitated and the situation may go from bad to worse.

Until you are very experienced, it is better to ride out in company. Licensed riding schools always escort hacks as their insurance policies do not cover unaccompanied riders on horses from their yards. If you should hack out on a friend's horse, find out whether the animal is insured and whether you are covered to ride him. You cannot risk injury or damage to yourself, the horse or to other people without having proper insurance. It is sensible always to carry enough money on you to make a phone call in case of emergencies, and a hoof pick. Always let someone know where you plan to ride on your hack and how long you expect to be. A riding school escort will obviously take care of all these aspects, as well as carrying some basic first aid equipment.

RIGHTS OF WAY

When riding out in the countryside, even if accompanied, you should know where and how you should ride. The public rights of way usually open to riders are bridle-paths or 'green lanes' which are old roads which have fallen into disuse. These paths are indicated on Ordnance Survey maps, as are footpaths which should not be used by riders. Even bridle-ways should be ridden with consideration for other users. Do not ride faster than a trot if you cannot see around a corner and always reduce your pace to walk if you are passing pedestrians. Ride in single file past walkers, do not crowd them into the hedgerow or crops, and remember to thank them if they have kept a dog under control as you pass. Be responsible about riding bridle-paths when ground conditions are wet – paths quickly become boggy if used indiscriminately. The owner of the land over which the path runs could close it altogether and be in no hurry to re-open it, even when conditions improve. Often farmers will allow riders known to them to ride over their land, around fields and along tracks which are not necessarily bridle-ways. Such permission should not be abused and, again, ground conditions always considered.

Take care when riding near crops to keep to the track. Learn to recognize the different cereal crops and know the difference between a field of young cereals and grass.

SAFETY

Always be careful when riding through or near fields stocked with cows or sheep. You should only ever walk through these fields as both cows and sheep can be easily panicked and you could start a stampede. Always make sure to shut gates behind you and learn to do this while mounted, though sometimes this is not possible. Check that your girth is as tight as possible before you get off, so the saddle does not slip on remounting. Cross the stirrups over the withers and take the reins over the pony's head to lead him through the gateway. Flapping stirrups could easily be caught in the gate and frighten the pony.

Learn to open and shut gates from the saddle but do make sure that any gate you open is shut again after you.

Flapping or bright articles in verges or hedgerows are usually startling for a horse. Keep your legs confidently at the horse's side and deepen your seat.

It is usual to ride with stirrups a little shorter for a hack than in the school, so if you have to dismount while out use a bank or a small wall to help you get back on again. It is important that the pony stands still while you remount and this again could cause problems if riding an unsuitable mount out on a hack.

Remember that ponies can take a dislike to almost anything which they consider potentially dangerous. Pigs are a common dislike, as are puddles, dustbins, dogs or baby buggies. Always try to keep looking straight ahead and keep a strong leg aid to send the pony past any obstacles. Keep talking calmly to the pony and praise him when you have got past the problem. Occasionally if you have a real difficulty, or if you yourself are posing a hazard to others, you should dismount, take the reins over the pony's head, cross the stirrups over the withers and lead him past gently and quietly, keeping between him and the problem.

Never venture out with tack which is old, worn or unsafe and always wear correct head and footgear. Cutting corners on safety is not worth the risk.

Few people nowadays are fortunate enough to be able to enjoy their riding without having to use the public highway. This provides probably the biggest hazard to horse and rider, not to mention the motorist. British Horse Society statistics show that eight road accidents a day involve horses and so those who venture onto the road with a horse should do everything they can to be as safe as possible.

Never consider any horse to be totally traffic-proof, although fortunately most prove themselves to be steady and reliable in all kinds of conditions. Until you are very experienced, do not take an inexperienced or unreliable pony onto the roads as you create danger for yourself and other road users. Such animals should always be ridden by experienced riders and, if possible, in the company of other, steadier horses.

However safe you consider your pony to be, remember that you also rely on the consideration of motorists. Riders can encourage drivers to take care when passing horses by making sure that acknowledgement is always given to those who do slow down. Drivers easily become annoyed when their courtesy is ignored or greeted by a blank stare. While it may be dangerous for you to take a hand off the reins to say thank you, a nod and a smile will do just as well. If you are riding towards a bend around which you can see and the driver cannot, do not make him impatient but indicate to him whether the road ahead is clear for him to pass or whether you can see another vehicle approaching. If possible, move into a gateway or onto the verge to allow him to pass.

HAZARDS ON THE ROADS

Sometimes ponies which are perfectly sensible with cars object to larger vehicles, buses or lorries. Whether they are approaching from behind or in front, keep the pony's head inclined slightly towards the vehicle and your right leg firmly on the girth. If he does shy away, he will move away from the vehicle and not into it.

It is always better to avoid hazards and any likely confrontations with your pony. Use your eyes, ears and common sense to anticipate problems and try to find another route if possible. If you have to pass road works or a dustbin lorry, halt for a moment in the hope that those working at the 'hazard' will

When negotiating a stationary hazard on the road, turn the horse's head away and keep the inside leg strong to keep him going forward. Keep your own attitude firm and keep looking ahead.

notice you and stop to let you pass. Even if you do not antici-pate a problem with your pony, it is still good practice to reassure him and ride straight forward, keeping the right leg working against the horse's side to prevent his quarters from swinging out into the traffic. If there is oncoming traffic, allow that to pass before negotiating a stationery hazard. If you take your time and talk quietly to your pony while riding positively forward he should respond accordingly. If you yourself be-come nervous, you will transmit this to the pony and this could well create a problem that might not otherwise have existed. If your pony refuses to face a hazard and you have other equine company, allow him to follow a steadier horse through. If you are on your own in difficult circumstances, it may be necessary for you to dismount and lead your pony past by taking the reins over his head, crossing the stirrups and leading him on your left-hand side, putting yourself between him and the traffic. In most circumstances, however, you are safer mounted and should dismount only if it is essential.

SAFETY CONSIDERATIONS

Always ride on the left side of the road and never ride on pavements, which will endanger pedestrians. Do not ride on mown verges that obviously belong to private houses, but if the roadside verge on country roads or lanes is wide enough, take advantage of this and leave the road free for cars. Avoid main roads at busy times, whether or not your horse is safe in traffic. Expecting motorists to queue behind you when they are rushing on their way to work does little to foster good rider/ driver relationships. Never make any manoeuvre without sig-nalling your intentions to other road users. Like riding a bike, always look back over your shoulder to check what is coming from behind, and then indicate with clear hand signals and, in good time, what you intend to do. Most signals and moves are similar to those you would make on a bike or in a car, except the right turn when you should keep to the left of the road until you make your turn, rather than moving out into the middle.

If possible, avoid riding in poor light. A motorist can see less well through his windscreen in morning and evening twilight than you can see out in the open. If it is necessary to ride at

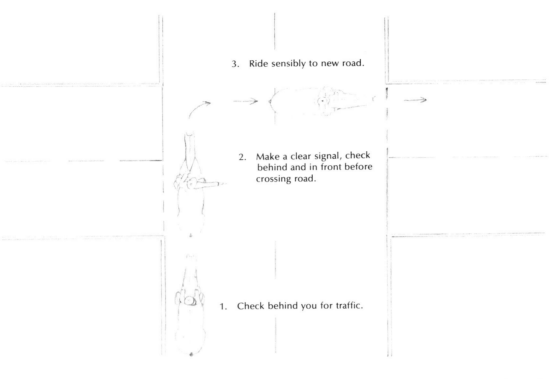

3. Ride sensibly to new road.

2. Make a clear signal, check behind and in front before crossing road.

1. Check behind you for traffic.

The correct way to make a right turn.

It is essential that drivers can see you, especially if you have to ride in bad light. This rider has a reflective tabard and stirrup light and has fitted her pony with reflective boots on the offside.

these times, wear as much light-reflective material on yourself and your pony as possible. You can wear a tabard or braces, as well as a reflective silk for your skull cap, while your horse can be fitted with boots, noseband and special rein grips. Stirrup lights showing white to the front and red to the rear give still more protection. Remember none of this will show up in fog or heavy mist and it is extremely dangerous for all road users to take your horse out in such conditions. Snow and frost are also to be avoided but when slippery road surfaces are slow to clear, or if the tarmac surface is shiny and slippery anyway, riding in close to the verge where small stones and grit remain gives extra purchase for your pony's feet. Worn horse shoes are a potential hazard, especially when the road surface is slippery, and you should not ride out if the pony is in need of new shoes.

Always make sure your pony's footwear is in good repair. The worn shoe on the right will easily slip on the road.

TAKE YOUR TEST

One of the best steps you can take as part of your riding education is to take the equivalent of the driving test – the British Horse Society's Riding and Road Safety Certificate. The tests are organized by the BHS or Pony Club and you could make enquiries at your riding school. The test is of the rider's roadcraft and ability, and is made up of a theory test, a simulated road route in the riding school and a road test on the public highway. A thorough inspection of tack and turnout is also made.

Whether or not you do take a test, you should be familiar with the Highway Code with regard to horses on the road, should be courteous to and have consideration for other road users at all times and should never take unnecessary risks.

As you become more experienced you will no doubt have the opportunity to ride out in the country. The varying terrains you will find, together with different ground conditions mean that you should extend your skills and knowledge so that at all times you can ride with the safety and consideration of your pony in mind.

Before you attempt any sort of energetic riding across country, you should have sufficient knowledge to decide whether your pony is fit enough to work in this way. Riding school ponies are looked after by experts and have enough work to keep them fit but if you are to ride a horse or pony which has little work during the week you should work him steadily and consistently in walk and trot before doing any cantering. Build this up gradually and when your pony does not appear to be tired or puffing and sweating after increasing periods of work, then you can be fairly sure that he is fit for what you want to do. Never put a pony to any unfamiliar work if you are unsure of his fitness and if you do not know, do not be afraid to ask for experienced help. Make sure that the pony's feet are regularly trimmed and shoes are not allowed to wear down as this can place extra strain on the horse's legs over conditions which demand fit, strong legs and feet.

Riding up hills is one of the best ways of getting a horse fit. It expands the lungs and develops the back and quarter muscles (think how you feel when you walk up a hill you are not used to). By gradually increasing the amount of hill work your pony will find it less effort, providing you continue to watch for signs of stress.

RIDING UPHILL

During uphill work in any pace, you should sit forward and get off the horse's back, so he takes your weight onto his shoulders, thus freeing his quarters to push up the hill. It is good exercise for you to shorten the stirrups by two or three holes and stand up jockey-style but you should be sufficiently secure to balance yourself over the horse's back and not be pulling back on the reins to maintain the position. If you stay in rising trot uphill, tilt your body slightly further forward than normal and stay very light as you sit in the saddle. As when jumping, the horse needs to stretch his head and neck while trotting or

When riding up a hill or bank take your weight forward more onto the pony's shoulder thus freeing his back and quarters to push up the hill.

cantering uphill and you should allow as much as possible without losing contact. Should he trip you must be in a position to sit up quickly and help him to regain his feet.

RIDING DOWNHILL

When riding downhill it is important to take a position slightly behind the vertical to help the horse balance. In good conditions on a balanced pony you can canter or gallop downhill but there is always a danger of the horse striking into a front leg with a hind leg, particularly if the ground is boggy or the grass slippery. On very steep banks you should proceed carefully, positioning your body well back. Approach in walk and gently urge the pony to step down, allowing him plenty of

When riding down a hill or steep bank, keep your weight well back to help the pony balance himself.

rein. Do not panic the pony into making a great leap from top to bottom or you may part company before you get down. In negotiating such hazards, it is always helpful to have another more experienced rider with you to act as a lead.

WATER

It is fun to splash through streams but make sure your entrance and exit are safe and that the stream bed is not flinty or slippery.

Water provides a hazard for some horses but it is fun to be able to splash through streams or rivers and is a nuisance if a horse has an aversion to it. If you are going to ride through a river, or even a big puddle in the road, you should be sure that the bottom is firm, not slippery, and the water not likely suddenly to become deep. If descending a bank into a stream, make sure it gives a clear, safe approach with no overhanging trees.

Horses sometimes dislike going from light into shade or vice versa and sunlight glistening on water may seem alarming to your pony, so always try to make sure the conditions are favourable if you are not sure how he will react.

Entry into water may be boggy and any heavy going should be treated with great caution. Shoes can very easily be pulled off and legs strained by thoughtless riding in such conditions. Try to avoid such situations altogether, but if it is necessary to ride through them, do so at a walk only.

If you are lucky enough to live near the sea, the beach gives you a wonderful natural 'all weather' riding surface which is put to good use by some racehorse trainers. Make sure you know the beach – whether the sand gets loose and soft or barely covers a rocky base – particularly before doing any fast work. Riding just at the water's edge provides the best surface while the small amount of resistance that the water itself gives helps to tone the horse's legs. Always have consideration for other beach users and beware of litter they may have left behind, especially cans and ring pulls.

If you are lucky enough to live near the sea, the beach gives a wonderful all-weather arena.

CANTERING ACROSS COUNTRY

The fastest pace at which you will have ridden within the confines of the riding school is the working canter. In jumping lessons you will have learnt how to sit up off the horse's back while cantering and this is the position you should adopt when cantering across country. If you have difficulty getting a canter in the school, you will find it much easier when riding out; but do not just follow the person in front. Apply the correct aid and feel that you have achieved something yourself. Next time you will find it easier in the school. When you are more experienced and if conditions allow, you can push your pony into a gallop, which is a four-time version of the canter and covers yet more ground with each stride. Again, keep up off his back and keep a steady contact on the rein. Riding in the countryside at faster paces is exciting for the horse so do make sure you are not riding beyond your capabilities. Do not forget always to check your girth before riding at faster paces.

Joining accompanied rides from riding schools, or perhaps on holiday from trekking centres on sensible, well-schooled horses and ponies will help you further your experience in a safe, more constructive way. If you should be riding on your own in unfamiliar surroundings, always bear in mind that fields or other open areas may be undermined by burrowing animals and stepping in a hole at a canter or gallop can lead to an accident. Be careful about riding over stony or flinty paths and only ever negotiate these at a walk. Your pony could slip, trip, or injure a foot or leg if you do not treat these conditions with care.

Once you have done a little bit of jumping, a small log or ditch is always tempting, but first make sure it is safe on take-off and landing and if you have any doubts about your ability, wait until you are more experienced.

Always remember that you have a responsibility for the health and welfare of any horse or pony you ride. If you consider the pony first it will help you keep risks to a minimum.

Before selecting a riding school, you need to know what you should look for in a good school and what the school can offer in the way of suitable horses and instruction.

In more highly populated areas there is a much greater choice of establishment than in rural areas, but before booking lessons at the one nearest you, try to visit a selection to see which is the best for you. The best instruction need not be the most expensive but riding is not a cheap sport and it is unlikely that the cheapest lessons you find would be the best. First obtain lists of riding schools approved by either the Association of British Riding Schools or the British Horse Society as this will be the first assurance that the schools are visited annually and their standards reassessed by inspectors from these organizations. All riding schools should at the very least have a local authority licence which means that they are inspected annually by an authorized veterinary surgeon. You should be very wary of any school which operates without such a licence as riding schools are legally obliged to have substantial public liability insurance. Any establishment which gives lessons to the public on school horses but does not have a

A neat tidy yard gives a good impression and shows a high standard of management.

licence is breaking the law and may not have adequate insurance cover.

STANDARDS OF INSTRUCTION

Having obtained your lists, look for the standards of instruction offered. The bigger schools usually train career students and will probably have the highest-qualified instruction. Often beginner riders are taught by student instructors and standards can vary greatly. You need to find out who would be teaching you and how experienced they are. Sometimes older teachers may not have any qualifications but their years of experience more than compensate. You or your parents could speak to clients of the school and ask them how they find the lessons and the standards generally.

Decide whether the ponies look well kept and how the riders seem to manage them.

FACILITIES

Do not necessarily be swayed by lavish facilities. Although impressive, they give no indication of the standard of instruction. Look for adequate, safe facilities and good instruction. Look also at the ponies and horses belonging to the school and decide whether they look well kept and how they behave themselves in the lessons. Do the other riders seem to have problems with them or are they basically well schooled? It is very hard to learn to ride on an inadequately schooled pony.

As you watch lessons in progress you will probably be able to choose which instructor appeals to you by the fun and education the riders are getting. Teaching and instructing have slightly different meanings and you should actually learn and benefit from an instructor who actually *teaches* you something new each time, rather than an instructor who merely instructs you to make various movements around the school.

Learning to ride should be fun and making the right decision about your teacher and school means that you will learn more quickly and enjoyably. If you make the wrong choice to start with, do not be afraid to change.

British Horse Society
British Equestrian
  Centre
Stoneleigh
Kenilworth
Warwickshire
CV8 2LR

Association of British
  Riding Schools
Old Brewery Yard
Penzance
Cornwall
TR18 2SL

A lesson in progress in a well-fenced manège. The pony looks willing and enthusiastic in his work over accurately-placed trotting poles. All riding facilities and instruction should, first and foremost, be safe.

Two items of clothing are essential for your first lesson: a correctly fitting hard hat and suitable footwear. Other items can be added later when you are riding regularly.

HARD HATS

Riding without proper headgear is foolhardy and no proper riding school would ever permit you to ride without a hard hat. Sixteen per cent of injuries to riders are head injuries and over seventy per cent of these could be reduced or avoided if correct headgear were worn.

Two types of hat are available, both conforming to British Standards and bearing the kite mark. The better is BS4472, the 'jockey skull', which has a fitted three-point chin harness. You can choose which colour silk to wear on top but if you progress to Pony Club events or shows and competitions it is usual to wear black or blue. The traditional velvet hard hat (BS6473) with flexible peak should also be worn with a three-point harness.

Whichever type of hat you choose, it must fit and the inner lining should be correctly adjusted to leave a gap between the top of your head and the inner surface of the hat. Unless this is done the hat will not act correctly as a shock absorber.

Hats do not last forever and should be looked after. If you have a fall in which your hat receives a knock, you should buy a new hat, as the damaged one will not withstand another knock. Be careful about where you put it down and do not drop it.

A hat will not serve its purpose unless it is on your head at the moment of impact. The chin harness should therefore always be fastened when riding.

RIDING BOOTS

Correct footwear is essential to prevent your foot slipping right through the iron or getting caught up in it in the event of a fall. Both would result in your being dragged and it is for this reason that the 'safety' bars on the saddle should not be closed.

Trainers, flat-soled shoes and wellington boots are not suitable for riding. Jodphur boots, rubber riding boots or, best

Casual clothes are fine but a hard hat and proper boots are essential.

of all, full-length leather boots are the only correct footwear, the main criterion being a deep heel. Should you need to have riding boots repaired, make sure that a full sole is fitted as a flapping half sole could result in an accident. The great advantage of full-length leather boots is that they protect your lower leg from kicks by other horses.

ITEMS FOR COMFORT

Most trousers are reasonably comfortable to ride in, but jeans tend to be too restrictive of movement and their thick seams can chafe your legs. Jodhpurs (full-length) and breeches (calf-length, to be worn with long boots) provide extra protection where it is needed and are usually made from stretch fabric. Different colours are available and these are practical but beige is the only really correct colour for more formal wear.

Hands, legs and feet can get very cold when riding in the winter. Two or three thinner, loose layers of clothes which trap in warm air are better than thick, heavy clothes. Do not wear thick socks which make your boots tight; cotton or lightweight wool socks are best, or a pair of nylon tights and thin socks on top. Leather boots provide greater warmth than rubber.

Tight jodhpurs, even 'thermal' ones, do not keep your thighs warm so wear tights underneath or leg warmers on top. Better still, leather chaps keep the chilling winds off your legs and keep you really warm.

For lessons and hacks, casual shirts and coats are perfectly all right, but never ride with a coat flapping open as this may frighten the horse. For Pony Club events or shows, wear a white or blue shirt and tie. A tweed hacking jacket completes more formal wear. For some show classes and competitions a black or blue jacket would be correct and you should check on this before entering particular classes.

Gloves should always be worn to prevent your fingers from blistering on the reins and to help you keep a more secure hold on the reins. Some horses continually lean on the reins which gradually get longer and longer. Wearing gloves will help you to prevent this from happening.

Protect your ears with a head scarf worn under your hat or a neck scarf pulled well up and keep the rest of your body warm under a light but warm 'holofill' duvet coat.

Change the rein Change direction, from the right to the left rein or vice versa. This can be done in several ways:
1. *across the diagonal* Between K-M or F-H, passing through X.
2. *across the centre of the school* E-X-B or B-X-E.
3. *down the centre line* A-X-C or C-X-A.

Check your diagonal (or just 'diagonal') In rising trot you should sit when the horse's outside shoulder comes back towards you. If you are on the wrong diagonal, sit for one extra stride.

Circle in the centre of the school A circle starting at E or B with X as the centre.

Inside rein The rein which corresponds with the inner bend of the horse, usually nearer the centre of the school.

Keep your distance (or watch your distances) Leave about one horse's or pony's length between you and the rider in front.

Leading file The rider in front; leading file in succession means one after the other.

Make much Pat your horse.

Move forward to . . . All changes of pace, or transitions, are ridden forward, even downward transitions, i.e. trot to walk, walk to halt.

Near side The left side of the horse.

Off side The right side of the horse.

On the left rein Anti-clockwise around the school.

On the right rein Clockwise around the school.

Outside rein Whichever rein you are on, the one which corresponds with the outside bend of the horse (usually nearer the outside of the school).

Prepare to . . . Before a command, the instructor gives you time to prepare for whatever the next movement is, e.g. prepare to move forward to rising trot, or working trot rising.

Prove your position Put a hand on the pommel and pull yourself down, so you are sitting deeply in the saddle.

Quit and cross your stirrups Take your feet out of the stirrups and cross the leathers in front of the saddle, so the left iron crosses to the right and vice versa. You will do this before riding without stirrups.

Shorten the reins Make the length of rein between your hand and the horse's mouth short enough to give you a 'feel' or elastic contact with the horse's mouth.

The ride   All the riders; also 'whole ride' and 'as a ride', meaning altogether.

The track   Around the outside of the school.

To the rear of the ride   Ride alone around the school and join again at the back.

Track right (or left)   On reaching the track, go to the right (or left).

Turn in and halt   Turn off the track at right angles and halt.

3-loop serpentine   A 'double S' starting at A or C.

20-metre circle   This usually means a circle covering half of the school you are in, touching the track at C or A and passing through X.

British Horse Society
British Equestrian Centre
Stoneleigh
Kenilworth
Warwickshire CV8 2LR

Association of British Riding Schools
Old Brewery Yard
Penzance
Cornwall TR18 2SL

British Show Hack, Cob and Riding Horse
  Association
Rookwood
Packington Park
Meriden
Warwickshire CV7 7HF

British Show Jumping Association
British Equestrian Centre
Stoneleigh
Kenilworth
Warwickshire CV8 2LR

Farriers Registration Council
PO Box 49
East of England Showground
Peterborough
Cambridgeshire PE2 0GU

Horses and Ponies Protection Association
64 Station Road
Padiham
Lancashire BB12 8EF

Hunters Improvement and National Light
  Horse Breeding Society
96 High Street
Edenbridge
Kent

National Pony Society
Brook House
25 High Street
Alton
Hampshire GU34 1AW

Ponies Association of UK
Chesham House
Green End Road
Sawtry
Huntingdon
Cambridgeshire PE17 5UY

Riding for the Disabled Association
Avenue R
National Agricultural Centre
Stoneleigh
Kenilworth
Warwickshire CV8 2LY

American Farriers Association
4089 Iron Works Pike
Lexington
KY 40511

American Grandprix Association
PO Box 495
Wayne
PA 19087

American Horse Council
1700 K St., NW
Suite 300
Washington DC 20006

American Horse Protection Association
1000 29th St., NW #T–100
Washington DC 20007

American Horse Shows Association
220 E 42nd Street
Suite 409
New York
NY 10017

North American Riding for the
Handicapped Association
PO Box 33150
Denver
CO 80233

United States Combined Training
Association
292 Bridge Street
South Hamilton
MA 01982

United States Dressage Federation
PO Box 80668
Lincoln
NE 68501

United States Pony Clubs
893 Matlock St., #110
West Chester
PA 19382

FURTHER READING

The Pony Club Manual of Horsemanship
Drummond, M   *The Horse Care and Stable Manual*
Foster, C   *The Athletic Horse*
Harris, C   *Fundamentals of Riding*
Houghton-Brown, J and Powell-Smith, V   *Horse and Stable Management*
Mairinger, F   *Horses are Made to be Horses*
Podhajsky, A   *The White Stallions of Vienna*
Rose, M   *The Horseman's Notebook*
Swift, C   *Centred Riding*

(Page numbers in italics refer to illustrations.)